EXTINCT UNDERWATER CREATURES

and those in danger of extinction

Philip Steele

Franklin Watts
New York London Toronto Sydney

© 1991 Franklin Watts

First published in the United States
by Franklin Watts
387 Park Avenue South
New York, N.Y. 10016

Design: Julian Holland Publishing Ltd
Picture research: Val Randall
Illustrator: Robert Morton

Printed in the United Kingdom

Library of Congress Cataloging-in-Publication Data

Steele, Philip.
    Extinct Underwater creatures/
by Philip Steele.
        p.   cm.–(Extinct).
    Includes index.
    Summary: Features the most famous
and unusual extinct or endangered
underwater plants and animals, explaining
when and how certain ones became
extinct.
    ISBN 0-531-11029-X
    1. Extinction (Biology) – Juvenile
literature. 2. Aquatic animals – Juvenile
literature. 3. Extinct animals – Juvenile
literature. 4. Aquatic plants – Juvenile
literature. 5. Plants – Extinction – Juvenile
literature. [1. Marine biology. 2. Rare
animals. 3. Extinct animals. 4. Rare plants.
5. Extinct plants.] I. Title. II. Series:
Extinct (Series)

QH78.S74 1992   91-10941
                        CIP AC

Photograph acknowledgments
p10 Museum fur Naturkunde, Berlin,
11 Peter Scoones/Planet Earth Pictures,
17 Hans Reinhard/Bruce Coleman Ltd,
18 Christian Petron/Planet Earth Pictures,
19 Ken Lucas/Planet Earth Pictures,
20 Zig Lescynski/Oxford Scientific Films,
21 B & C Calhoun/Bruce Coleman Ltd,
22 Allan Power/Bruce Coleman Ltd,
23 WWF & J Trotignon/Bruce Coleman
Ltd, 24 Andrea Florence/Ardea London,
25 Heather Angel, 26 Ferrero/
Greenpeace, 27 F Gohier/Ardea London.

Contents

Death in the lake

Most of our planet is covered in water. Its oceans, seas, lakes, rivers and streams are home to a vast number of aquatic creatures. Some are invertebrates, simple animals without backbones such as corals, sponges and shellfish. Others are vertebrates, animals whose bodies are supported by backbones. These animals include fish, amphibians such as frogs and newts, reptiles such as sea snakes, and mammals such as seals and whales. Many birds are also at home in water, diving, swimming or wading.

Some underwater creatures live in fresh water, while others prefer the salty water of the sea. However, many of our seas and lakes are dying because of the actions of people, and the survival of many aquatic creatures is at risk.

1937 Lake trout introduced to Lake Titicaca.
1950 Titicaca orestias on the verge of extinction.

The Titicaca orestias

Lake Titicaca lies high in the Andes mountains of South America, on the border between Bolivia and Peru. For hundreds of years, the Uru Indians have caught fish in the shallow waters of the lake. In the past they also landed a fish which lived in the chilly depths of the lake – the Titicaca orestias.

However, the Uru Indians are unlikely to catch many Titicaca orestias today. In 1937, lake trout were introduced into Lake Titicaca. The competition proved too great for the Titicaca orestias because the lake trout live and feed at the same depth as them and the trout upset the food balance.

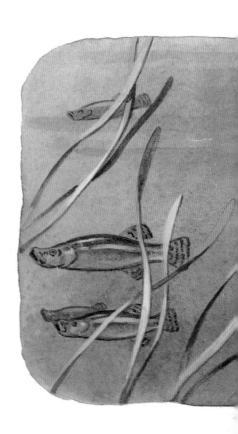

The Titicaca orestias is now listed as endangered by the International Union for the Conservation of Nature and Natural Resources (IUCN), and may soon disappear altogether, or become extinct. Relatives of the Titicaca orestias, such as the Parras pupfish and the perritos de sandia of Mexico, have already become extinct.

DID YOU KNOW?
- The Titicaca orestias belongs to a large family of which 11 types, or species, are endangered, and 11 are vulnerable. Three species are listed as very rare.
- About 350 major species of fish are listed on the Red List of Threatened Animals published by the IUCN.

▼ *Umatos* is the local name for the Titicaca orestias, the largest of several related scaly fish called tooth carps. Greenish brown and black, the adult fish can grow up to 26.5 cm (10.5 in) in length.

Long ago

The first fish developed, or evolved, in the sea about 450 million years ago. They were the first vertebrates. Many were protected by armor plating, but had no jaws or teeth. By 295 million years ago, new kinds of fish were evolving, which were more like the fish we know today. Some fish developed powerful front fins to haul themselves from one muddy pool to another. These fish evolved into the first amphibians, animals whose way of life is suited to both water and land.

The amphibians continued to develop and adapt to their surroundings, or environment. Over millions of years, the world's climate and vegetation changed. Seas were formed and dried up again. Animals that could not adapt became extinct. Reptiles and mammals appeared. These animals lived on dry land and breathed air into their lungs. Some mammals and reptiles returned to live in the sea, like their ancestors. Whales are mammals that have become so suited to a life underwater that they even look like fish.

350 million years ago: *Dunkleosteus* alive. 300 million years ago: *Xenacanthus* alive. 15 million years ago: great shark alive.

▼ *Xenacanthus* was an early kind of shark. Like the sharks of today, its skeleton was made of gristle, or cartilage, instead of bone. It lived in freshwater lakes and pools, and hunted smaller fish. It grew to 70 cm (28 in) in length.

DID YOU KNOW?
- The largest extinct fish was the great shark. Some of its teeth have been found in California, and they are 127 mm (5 in) long. This would suggest that the fish's body may have measured over 13 m (43 ft) from snout to tail fin.

▲ At 9 m (30 ft) long, *Dunkleosteus* was a fish the size of a school bus. Its other name was *Dinichthys,* which means "terrible fish." Its monstrous mouth was lined with jagged, bony plates, and it used these to crack open the armored bodies of other fish.

Fossils

When prehistoric creatures died, many sank to the bottom of the lakes and seas where their bones were covered with soft mud. Later, the mud hardened into rock. The remains and traces of plant and animals life left in stone are called fossils.

Today, fossils are often found in rocks that are now far from the sea. The "fossil record" includes all kinds of aquatic creatures, including sea urchins, starfish, fish and reptiles. When scientists study fossils, they can work out how individual creatures lived and what they ate.

Mosasaurus

In 1770, a strange-looking fossil was dug from chalk rocks near Maastricht in the Netherlands. Later it was taken to the Museum of Natural History in Paris where it was studied and recognized as the skull of the sea lizard, *Mosasaurus.* This marine reptile lived in shallow seas and became extinct at the same time as the dinosaurs.

100 million years ago: *Kronosaurus* alive. 70 million years ago: *Mosasaurus* alive.

▶ *Mosasaurus* was about 12 m (39 ft) in length. It swam through the water by moving its tail from side to side. Its limbs were like paddles, and its long jaws were packed with large, sharp teeth.

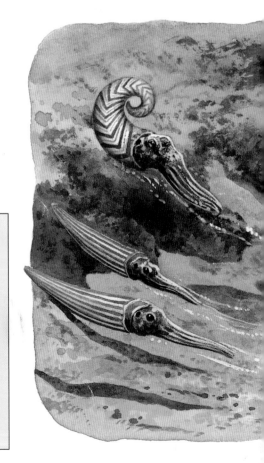

DID YOU KNOW?
- *Mosasaurus* ate fish and free-swimming mollusks called ammonites. Some ammonite fossils found today show the tooth marks of *Mosasaurus.*
- Fossil remains of sea lizards have been found all over the world. Relatives of *Mosasaurus* include *Tylosaurus* and *Kronosaurus*.
- The largest marine reptile fossil ever recorded was a *Kronosaurus,* which measured 15.2 m (50 ft) in length.

A living fossil

Fossils of coelacanth species have been found that date back over 405 million years. Scientists can tell from the fossils that the coelacanths were heavy-bodied, scaly fish with powerful fins. They also know that in fish like the coelacanth, the lungs of earlier species evolved into sacs of air. These "swim-bladders" helped the fish control the way they floated in the water.

Everyone thought that fish like these were extinct. Then in 1938, a species of coelacanth was caught in the Chalumna River, South Africa. A woman called Miss Latimer saw the fish and arranged for it to be sent to scientists for identification. It caused a sensation around the world. The scientists named the species *Latimeria*.

In 1952 another coelacanth was caught off the Comoro Islands in the Indian Ocean. More have been caught there since. Scientists are now trying to find out more about the way of life of these unusual fish.

405 million years ago: First coelacanths appear.
200 million years ago: Coelacanth species common.
65 million years ago: Once thought to be the date at which coelacanths became extinct.
1938 *Latimeria* found off South Africa.

▼ Perfectly preserved in stone, this fossil shows the stocky, blunt-headed shape of a coelacanth. Only now do we know that relatives of fish like these are still swimming in our seas.

- The name "coelacanth" means "hollow-spined." Fossils show that its fin spines are made of hollow cartilage, or gristle.
- Today's surviving coelacanth, *Latimeria* is listed as a threatened species by the IUCN. Because the depths where the fish lives are hard to explore, little is known about how many survive. It is certainly very rare and faces an uncertain future.

▲ *Latimeria* is a deep-sea dweller and is normally found at depths of up to 400 m (1,300 ft). It weighs about 90 kg (200 lb) and has a slimy body, which is either brown or blue. *Latimeria* gives birth to live young.

Enemies of nature

Until 150 years ago, people caught only enough fish and animals to keep themselves alive. During the nineteenth century, however, they began to hunt and fish on a vast scale, and many species of whale, fish and seal were in danger of becoming extinct.

Men and women traveled by ship to remote places and settled in new lands. Often the settlers introduced new species of animals to a region, and these destroyed the creatures already living there.

The grayling tragedy

In the nineteenth century, many European settlers arrived in New Zealand. They cut trees which shaded rivers, and stocked streams with species of trout that were new to the area. They fished for food and sport, and one of the most popular game fishes was the New Zealand grayling. It used to be a common fish, but by the beginning of the century it was very rare, and by 1923 it was extinct.

▼ The New Zealand grayling had silvery to russet scales, and could grow to 50 cm (20 in) in length and weigh 1.4 kg (3 lb). The fish preferred to live in swiftly flowing rivers and streams.

In recent years, we have polluted the sea with sewage, oil and chemical waste. Rivers and lakes have been filled with poisons from factories and farms. Chemicals from power plants and exhaust fumes from cars rise into the air and later fall as acid rain. This acid rain has killed freshwater fish in their thousands.

▲ The Australian grayling is a relative of the New Zealand species, and it is in danger of suffering the same fate as its cousin. It lives in rivers along the coast of south-east Australia and Tasmania. It has been killed by river pollution, by the building of dams and weirs, and by overfishing.

DID YOU KNOW?
- In 4,000 Swedish lakes all forms of life have been destroyed by acid rain.
- One of the worst oil spills ever recorded happened off the island of Tobago in July 1979. Two super tankers, the *Atlantic Express* and the *Aegean Captain,* collided and 236,000 tons of oil were spilled into the sea.

1923 New Zealand grayling extinct.
1988 Australian grayling listed as vulnerable.

The cisco story

The Great Lakes lie on the border between Canada and the United States. The lakes are called Superior, Michigan, Huron, Erie and Ontario and cover a total area of 246,000 sq km (95,000 sq mi). The lakes were formed by glaciers during the last Ice Age, and for thousands of years provided a home for fish, waterbirds and beavers. The American Indians fished and hunted animals around the lakes, but after the arrival of the Europeans in the region 300 years ago, fish stocks were reduced in disastrous numbers.

During the nineteenth and twentieth centuries, industrial cities were built on the shores of the lakes. Poisons from the factories in the cities polluted the waters.

Fish numbers were also reduced by fishing. All summer long the fishermen's nets hauled in shoals of ciscos, or "lake herring" as they were commonly known. In winter the fish were caught through the ice. If too many were caught, they were simply thrown away. By the turn of the century fish stocks were running low in Lakes Michigan, Huron and Erie. As species became rare, some were finally made extinct by the sea lamprey, a greedy sucker-mouthed fish which had been introduced to the lakes.

Fished to extinction

The first casualties of the Great Lakes were the longjaw cisco and the deepwater cisco, relatives of the salmon. They were fished until there were none left, and were probably extinct by the 1960s.

DID YOU KNOW?
- During the 1885 fishing season 19 million tons of fish were caught in just one of the Great Lakes.
- Other fish in the Great Lakes are also in danger of becoming extinct. These include the rare cisco and its relatives, the blackfin, shortnose and shortjaw cisco, the bloater, the kiyi and the Atlantic whitefish.

1910 Cisco species in decline.
1960 Cisco species endangered or extinct.

▶ The deepwater cisco (below) was a herring-sized fish with large silvery scales and a short back or dorsal fin. It weighed about 1 kg (2.2 lb). The longjaw cisco (above) was a close relative with a streamlined body and snout.

Fish under threat

Before humans appeared on Earth, prehistoric species were threatened only by competition and changes in their environment. In modern times, especially during the last century, humans have caused the extinction of hundreds of species. How many water creatures will survive the next 100 years?

DID YOU KNOW?
- A female common sturgeon can lay over 2 million eggs.

The Mekong catfish
The Mekong River is 4,000 km (2,500 mi) long. It rises in the mountains of China and flows southwards through Laos, Thailand, Cambodia and Vietnam. It branches into many smaller rivers when it reaches the coast south-west of Ho Chi Minh City.

The Mekong and the rivers which flow into it are home to a giant catfish. It lives in the deeper parts of the rivers, but swims upstream to lay its eggs in lakes and shallows. The Mekong catfish has long been fished by humans, and is famous for its tasty flesh. Overfishing has led to its being threatened as a species, and those caught today are small. Fewer and fewer are being found.

▼ The Mekong catfish is about 2.5 m (8 ft) long. It has a deep, flattened body, a single pair of feelers, or barbels, and toothless jaws.

◄ The common sturgeon can weigh over 200 kg (441 lb) and grow to 3 m (10 ft) in length. It is a thin-bodied fish, with a bony back and barbels.

Sturgeons at risk

The common sturgeon is a fish of the European coastline which lives at sea but returns to rivers to lay its eggs. Both the eggs and fish have been eaten by humans since the Stone Age, but in modern times this sturgeon has become increasingly rare.

The common sturgeon is an endangered species. It has been overfished, poisoned by chemicals in rivers and barred from its breeding water by weirs and dams. Now it breeds only in one Spanish river, the Guadalquivir, in one French river, the Gironde, and in parts of eastern Europe.

There are 25 species of sturgeon, of which 7 are thought to be at risk.

THE EMPTYING OCEANS
- Modern oceangoing fleets use electronic equipment to track shoals of fish. It enables them to catch vast numbers. A single net cast off Norway once hauled in over 2,470 tons of fish — over 100 million individuals. Fish that were once common are now scarce.

Corals and shells

Fish are not the only aquatic creatures to be threatened by the modern world. Corals, sea anemones, starfish, sea urchins, fresh and saltwater shellfish and sponges are all at risk. Animals that filter tiny particles of food from the water are particularly in danger in waters that are polluted.

Corals suffer from two main threats. First they cannot thrive in heavily polluted waters. Second, they are taken in large numbers for souvenirs or to be carved into jewelry and ornaments. Of 20 precious coral species in the Mediterranean Sea and the Pacific Ocean, six are threatened by this multimillion dollar trade. When a coral reef has been plundered, it can take 50 years to recover.

▼ Corals look like plants, but are in fact groups of small, soft-bodied animals encased in a chalky skeleton. Pieces of the skeleton are broken off by divers or by trawlers that dredge the ocean floor. Then the corals are polished or carved and made into necklaces and earrings.

The giant clam

The group of animals called mollusks includes sea snails, squids and octopuses. Mollusks with twin shells joined by a hinge are called bivalves. The largest bivalve mollusk is the giant clam of the Indian and Pacific oceans.

Today, the numbers of giant clams are much reduced. The shells are taken by collectors, and are also used for garden ornaments and roof-tiling material. The flesh of the giant clam is eaten throughout the Pacific regions, especially in Japan.

Australia's Great Barrier Reef is now patrolled by aircraft to prevent the poaching of clams, but the giant clam and six related species are still at risk.

▲ The giant clam is a filter feeder which also digests tiny creatures that grow on its mantle, or shell lining. It can grow to a width of 137 cm (54 in) and weigh over 200 kg (441 lb).

DID YOU KNOW?
● Mediterranean coral was being traded in the Stone Age. The Romans, 2,000 years ago, realized the danger of over-collection.

Overfishing

Crustaceans include crabs, lobsters, shrimps and prawns, and freshwater crayfish. The smaller crustaceans provide food for fish and whales. The larger crustaceans are hunted by humans.

Once lobsters were used as a cheap source of food, for fishing bait or fertilizer. Now they are an expensive luxury. Over 150,000 tons of lobsters are caught around the world each year, and most of them are sold to restaurants and hotels. As prices have risen, lobsters have been overfished, and the size of individual specimens has become smaller. Boats have had to drop their traps farther and farther from the coast.

▼ An American lobster eating a herring. In the North Atlantic Ocean, the American lobster has been added to the world's list of species at risk, being classed as "commercially threatened."

Echinoderms

Creatures such as starfish, sea cucumbers and sea urchins are called echinoderms. Some echinoderms, like urchins, perform a useful function by keeping down the growth of algae and maintaining the balance in the underwater food chain.

Over 50,000 tons of echinoderms are caught each year, mainly to be eaten. Echinoderms are also sold to tourists as ornaments. Few sea urchins face extinction, but many are threatened. They have been overfished and destroyed by oil spillages and pollution.

▲ The purple sea urchin is found in the Mediterranean Sea and south of Cape Cod on the Atlantic Coast.

DID YOU KNOW?
● In 1934, a lobster weighing over 19 kg (42 lb) was caught off the coast of Virginia. Today, most lobsters weigh over 2 kg (4.5 lb).

Water mammals

Aquatic mammals are particularly at risk from human hunters. Many are large and have to come to the surface to breathe air. They are easily shot or harpooned near the surface. Some mammals, such as the dugong and the manatee, are under threat and could become extinct during the next 100 years.

The dugong

The dugong is a strange-looking creature that lives in the warm waters of the Red Sea and Indian and Pacific oceans. It has been hunted for its meat, and it is easily spotted as it moves through the floating water weeds. The Australian Aborigines hunted the dugong with spears. When Europeans settled in Australia they netted the dugong and found that they could extract up to 55 l (15 gal) of oil from a single carcass, and use this as a substitute for cod-liver oil.

▼ The dugong is about 3 m (10 ft) long, including its large, flattened tail. Its body is shaped like a torpedo and its squat head is designed for grazing water weeds from the seabed. The dugong's hide is thick and gray, and the male has large tusks.

   Along with many other marine creatures, the dugong was threatened by oil slicks during the Gulf War in 1991.

Seals

True seals have been hunted for their skins and flesh since the Stone Age. Until recently seal pups were clubbed to death on the ice floes of Canada, and their skins sold to the fur trade. As a result of being hunted by humans, the Saimaa seal of Finland is endangered and the Kuril seal of the Soviet Union is vulnerable. In other parts of the world, seals are also under threat. There are still a few thousand Hawaiian monk seals left, but only a few hundred Mediterranean monk seals.

▲ The Mediterranean monk seal is nearly 3 m (10 ft) long. It is gray-brown and has a white belly patch.

UNDER THREAT
Aquatic mammals whose survival is threatened include:
- 8 species of otter
- 3 species of fur seal
- 1 species of walrus
- the pygmy hippopotamus

Whales and dolphins

Whales and dolphins are among the most gentle and intelligent mammals on Earth. Twenty-one species are currently at risk. Dolphins are often caught in fishing nets or are poisoned by pollution. Whales are killed by the thousands for their flesh, fat and oil.

During the last century, whales were hunted by brave men in small, wooden boats. As the whales plunged and slapped their huge tails against the water, many boats were sunk and many of the men were killed. Today, the whalers use large steel ships that are equipped with harpoon guns and winches. No risks are taken and nothing is left to chance.

International laws now control whaling, and since 1986 hunting has been strictly limited. However, illegal whaling still takes place, and some species are so low in number that they may never recover. Even endangered species are still killed.

▼ The boto, or Amazon River dolphin, lives in the muddy waters of the Amazon and can grow to 2.6 m (8.5 ft) in length.

Since 1988 the boto has been protected because it is thought to be vulnerable, or likely to become endangered. In the past many were killed by settlers. The dolphins also got caught in fishing nets and were collected for aquaria.

The blue whale

The blue whale is the largest creature to have lived on Earth. Its summer feeding grounds are in cold, polar waters, where it swallows krill, a kind of small crustacean, by the ton. In winter it swims to warm, tropical waters to breed.

Between 1900 and 1966, when the hunting of blue whales was banned, about 340,000 of these giants were killed. The blue whale became an endangered species. Today's blue whale population is perhaps 10 percent of its level in the 1930s, but scientists are hopeful that it will increase. The sheer size of the blue whale makes it impossible to keep in captivity.

▲ The blue whale is a vast streamlined mammal that is found in all the world's oceans. Blue whales can weigh over 130 tons.

DID YOU KNOW?
- In 1930 to 1931 almost 300,000 blue whales were killed in the Antarctic alone.
- The largest blue whale on record measured over 33 m (108 ft).

Wildlife SOS

In the past, people did not realize that the earth's resources were limited, and that their actions were destroying whole species forever. Today, many people are working hard to protect endangered species and to help them to increase their numbers.

There are many ways in which action can be taken. Although there are laws that are meant to stop people hunting and fishing for endangered creatures, these are often not enforced. Also, more scientific research is needed to find out about threatened species and their habitats. Before tourist developments or major construction works are started the effect on wildlife should be taken into account first.

▼ Greenpeace is one of several international organizations that campaign for a better environment. Here a Greenpeace boat is trying to stop a whaling vessel making a kill.

In the last 25 years, there have been disastrous oil spillages from shipwrecked tankers which have destroyed all kinds of underwater life. Factories and farms have polluted rivers, and poisonous waste and sewage have been dumped in the sea. Acid rain can only be stopped by filtering the fumes from power plants and factories. This is expensive, and many countries cannot afford the changes. However, the problem is international and other countries must help.

▲ When salmon return to their breeding grounds, they leap over weirs and waterfalls which stand in their way. However, they cannot get past dams and grills. To help them bypass such obstacles, salmon "ladders" have been built in many places.

Glossary

acid rain Poisoned rainfall, formed when smoke and chemicals from factory or power plant chimneys rise into the atmosphere.

adapt To change or come to terms with new living conditions.

algae A group of plants including seaweeds and microscopic water growth.

amphibians Animals that have evolved so that part of their lives is spent on the water, and part on the land.

aquatic Living in water.

bivalve A mollusk that has a double shell joined by a hinge.

echinoderms Animals with bodies protected by calcite plates, such as sea urchins or starfish.

endangered At risk of becoming extinct.

environment The world in which a plant or animal lives, including the soil, climate, vegetation and air.

evolve To develop and adapt to changing living conditions.

extinct No longer living. Scientists now declare an animal to be extinct when it has not been seen in the wild for 50 years.

fossil The remains of an ancient animal or plant preserved in rock.

introduce To bring an animal species to live in an area where it does not normally breed.

invertebrate An animal without a backbone, such as an insect, a worm or a sponge.

mammals Warm-blooded animals that feed their young on milk. Most mammals give birth to live young and are covered in hair or fur.

pollution The poisoning of the air, soil or water by human activities such as industry or farming.

rare Scarce, uncommon.

reptiles Cold-blooded, egg-laying animals whose bodies are covered in scales.

species A single group of identical animals or plants.

vertebrate An animal with a backbone, such as a reptile, amphibian, bird or mammal.

vulnerable At risk of becoming an endangered species.

Find out more

- What can you do to save the aquatic creatures now under threat? The Wildlife Preservation Trust International sponsors the Dodo Club for young people. To find out more, write to the Trust at 34th Street and Gerard Avenue, Philadelphia, Pennsylvania 19104. Other campaigning organizations include Greenpeace, USA; 1436 U Street, N.W.; Washington, DC 20009; and Friends of the Earth; 530 Seventh Street, S.E.; Washington, DC 20009.

- Find out if your local naturalists' clubs and conservation groups need any help. They may be involved in cleaning up rivers and canals, or checking beaches for pollution. They may be checking local populations of otters and other aquatic creatures, or setting up nature reserves.

- Most big cities have a museum of natural history or science, where you can see fossils and reconstructions of prehistoric fish and marine reptiles. Some zoos and aquariums offer educational programs about aquatic wildlife.

Time chart

PREHISTORIC PERIOD		
Years ago	**Human history**	**Natural history**
3,500 million		First life appears in oceans.
390 million		First sharks evolve.
350 million		*Dunkleostus* alive.
300 million		*Xenacanthus* alive.
200 million		Coelacanths widespread.
100 million		*Kronosaurus,* longest marine reptile, alive.
80 million		*Elasmosaurus* alive. Sea birds hunt fish.
15 million		Great shark alive.
4 million	"Ape-people," such as *Australopithecus,* evolve.	
100,000	Modern people evolve, hunters with weapons of stone and bone.	

HISTORIC PERIOD		
10,000 B.C.	Humans hunt fish and waterfowl with finely crafted hooks and spears.	No threat to marine and freshwater species.
1500 B.C.- A.D. 800	Classical period in Europe followed by so-called Dark Ages. Commercial fishing, whale and seal hunting. Romans concerned at extent of coral collection.	Collection of coral. No overfishing or overhunting.
800-1450	Freshwater fish farmed in ponds. Commercial fishing and hunting. Building of weirs and obstacles on rivers.	Loss of habitat.
1450-1800	Europeans colonize foreign lands. Fishing, whaling, hunting of European and North American beaver, sealing. Drainage of wetlands. Angling becomes a popular hobby.	Loss of habitat. Species at risk. Steller's sea cow extinct (c1767).
1800-1900	Industry spreads across landscape. Pollution of rivers. Large-scale commercial fishing, whaling and sealing. Hunting of sea cows such as the dugong. Anglers introduce fish from one country to another. Growth of interest in natural history and evolution.	Loss of habitat. Species at risk. Three seabirds extinct.
1900-	Industrial pollution. Acid rain poisons lakes and rivers. Oil slicks at sea kill seabirds and fish. Overfishing and factory ships. Whaling on a vast scale. Introduction of fish species. Fish-farming. Growth of interest in conservation and ecology.	Loss of habitat. Twenty-three fish species extinct by 1988. Over 230 fish species at risk. Twenty-one species of whale and dolphin at risk. Nine species of seal and walrus at risk. Four species of sea cow at risk.

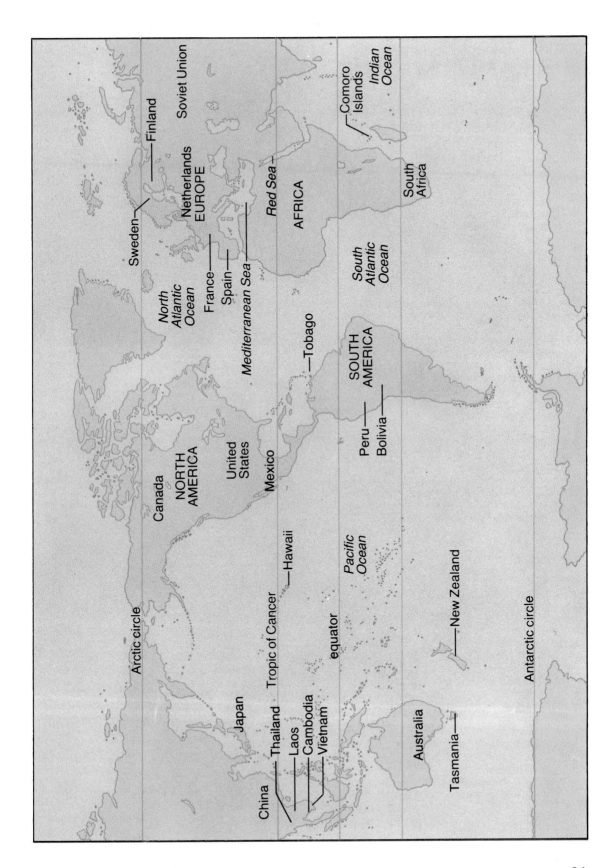

Index

mo